Hot Like Fire
and Other Poems

Poems from The World Is Sweet and Hot Like Fire by
Valerie Bloom

Illustrations by
Debbie Lush

BLOOMSBURY

LONDON BERLIN NEW YORK

Bloomsbury Publishing, London, Berlin and New York

The World Is Sweet first published in Great Britain in 2000 by
Bloomsbury Publishing Plc
Hot Like Fire first published in Great Britain in 2002 by
Bloomsbury Publishing Plc

This omnibus edition first published in Great Britain in 2009 by
Bloomsbury Publishing Plc, 36 Soho Square, London, W1D 3QY

A CIP catalogue record of this book is available from the British Library

ISBN 978 0 7475 9973 9

The paper this book is printed on is certified independently in
accordance with the rules of the FSC. It is ancient-forest friendly.
The printer holds chain of custody.

FSC
Mixed Sources
Product group from well-managed
forests and other controlled sources
Cert no. SGS - COC - 2061
www.fsc.org
© 1996 Forest Stewardship Council

Typeset by Dorchester Typesetting Group Ltd
Printed in Great Britain by Clays Ltd, St Ives Plc

1 3 5 7 9 10 8 6 4 2

www.bloomsbury.com/childrens
www.valbloom.co.uk

The World Is Sweet

For Gerry, Ian, Rochelle, Sarah, David and Pippa – VB

Hot Like Fire

To Peter, Sylvia, Maya and Imogen, with love – VB

To Giles – DL

Contents

The World Is Sweet

Frost

Overnight, a giant spilt icing sugar on the ground,
He spilt it on the hedgerows, and the trees without
   a sound,
He made a wedding-cake of the haystack in the
   field,
He dredged the countryside and the grass was all
   concealed,
He sprinkled sugar on the roofs, in patches not too
   neat,
And in the morning when we woke, the world
   around was sweet.

Seasons

Spring is a baby,
bright, fresh and new,
gurgling with the melting snow,
singing with the first cuckoo.

Summer is a barefoot boy,
fishing in the stream,
running through the waiting corn,
lazing in a dream.

Autumn's a grown man,
slowly walking by,
a limp in his careful footstep,
a shadow in one eye.

Winter is an aged sage,
with long, snow-powdered hair.
He cuts a trench in the frozen ground,
and buries another year.

Next Door's Cat

Next door's cat is by the pond,
Sitting, waiting for the fish,
Next door's cat thinks Geraldine
Would make a tasty dish.

He's had Twinkle and Rose Red,
He ate Alberta too,
And all we found were Junior's bones
When that horrid cat was through.

Next door's cat comes round at night,
Strikes when we're in bed,
In the morning when we wake,
Another fish is dead.

Next door's cat has seen the new fish,
He thinks that it's a goner,
What a surprise he's going to get,
When he finds it's a piranha.

Goldfish

You are trying to tell me something.
I see your mouth open and close,
An O sad as tears,
But I hear only the silence,
And an occasional apostrophe
Of despair.

The Old House

They say, in the night when the dogs take fright
And run howling from the streets,
When the hooded owl shrieks, and the wild wind
    wails,
And you lie shaking beneath the sheets,

They say, when the moon is too terrified
To play with the stones in the drive,
When bats bury their heads beneath their wings,
Then the old house comes alive.

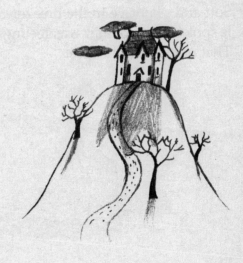

He came from a place near the sunset,
He went to a place without light,
He walked too late without company,
He walked too late at night.

He could have come early, at six or seven,
Or even later, at four or five,
But he chose to arrive at the very hour
That the old house came alive.

He heard that old house calling,
He had no power to say no,
He climbed up the hill, crossed over the bridge,
Though he knew that he shouldn't go.

Its voice was like a lost child's,
Soft and plaintive in the breeze,
It spoke of the pain it was feeling
That only he could ease.

It whispered to him in strange words
That no one else could hear,
Weird words that held such promises,
That would fill sane men with fear.

His head urgently whispered a caution,
'You'll turn back now if you are smart'.
But he had no will to listen,
For the house had hold of his heart.

He stepped on to the porch where the rotting
   boards creaked,
Through the door that beckoned, ajar,
Towards a light that flickered and peaked
Like a single, lonely star.

He heard the creaking door slam shut,
The festering floorboards sigh,
As in a dream, he thought, 'How sad,
I've come this far to die.'

They heard the scream, felt the anguish,
They knew he would not survive,
And they hear it still every night at twelve
When the old house comes alive.

Scared of the Dark

I'm scared of the dark
I don't like it one bit,
I'm scared of the dark,
There, I've admitted it.

I'm scared of the things
That go bump in the night
I'm scared of the creatures
Outside of the light.

I'm scared of the dark,
And what scares me the most,
Is when in the dark
I meet another ghost.

Jeremy Bishop

Jeremy, Jeremy Bishop,
Was a good boy, he ate all his fishop,
When he was done,
Like a well-brought up son,
He washed and dried his dishop.

My Brother Helps Out

Can I help you make the cake, Mum?
Please, let me, I know how,
I can do it, ple-ee-ee-ze! Oh thank you!
Let me have it. Right. What now?

Oh yes, I knew that, this is easy,
I'll be careful, I won't hurry,
Whisk it like this, right? I'm okay,
Honest I can do – oops! sorry.

Can I help you clean the windows?
Can I use the Windolene?
I'll not smudge it, I can do it,
C'mon, Mum, please, don't be mean.

Oh yes, I knew that, leave me to it,
I'll be careful, don't you worry,
Spray it like this, right? I'm all right,
Yes I'll mind your eyes – oops! sorry.

Can I help you mop the floor, Mum?
I have mopped the floor before,
Let me do it, 'cause I know that
You think mopping is a chore.

I'll be careful with the bucket,
There's no need for such a flurry,
Don't you trust me? I'll just put
The bucket on this stool – oops! sorry.

Are you making bread-rolls, Lucy?
Can I help you knead the dough?
I am nearly as old as you now,
So can I help you? Can I?
NO!

My Sister Tells a Joke

There was this man . . .
Now tell me if you've heard this one before.
Please Jonathan, come away from the bedroom
    door.

There was this man . . .
Or was it a boy? Doesn't really matter, I suppose,
Oh, Rachael! You shouldn't punch Jonathan on the
    nose!

There was this man . . .
Jonathan, I'm sure she didn't mean any harm.
Yes, Rachael, I remembered to set the alarm.

There was this man . . .
Rachael, you can't play that tape again!
Jon, what are you doing? Give me that fountain
    pen.

There was this man . . .
Will you two please listen to me!
That's better. Now where was I? Let me see

There was this man . . .
Hold on a minute; let me make sure I get this
   right,
Oh bother, here's Mum, come to turn out the light.

Rachael, here's your tape, Jonathan, take your pen,
Remind me never to try and tell you two a joke
   again.

Guidance

Wash yuh han' dem before yuh eat,
Sit still, teck yuh foot dem off the seat,
Don' scrape the plate with yuh knife an' fork,
An' keep quiet when big people a-talk,
Stop drag yuh foot dem pon the floor,
Ah tell yuh a'ready, don' slam the door,
Cover up yuh mout' when yuh a-cough,
Don' be greedy, give yuh sister half
O' the banana that yuh eatin' there,
What kind o' dress that yuh a-wear?
Don' kiss yuh teeth when me talk to yuh,
An' mind how yuh lookin' at me too,
Teck me good advice, me girl,
Manners carry yuh through the worl',
Ah tellin' yuh all this fe yuh own good,
Yuh should thank me, show some gratitude.

Life is very tough for me,
When Uncle Henry comes to tea.

Next Door's Cat – 2

Next door's cat ate my piranha,
He ate it for a lark,
I've put a new fish in the pond,
And this time it's a shark.

Something Comes

Over the mountains,
Like thunder of drums,
Shaking the leaves from trees,
Something comes.

Down through the valleys
With the bellow of bombs,
Alarming the cows and sheep,
Something comes.

Up through the forests,
The frightened air hums,
For tearing it in pieces,
Something comes.

Moving up the driveway
With a noise that numbs,
Crumpling the paving stones
Something COMES!

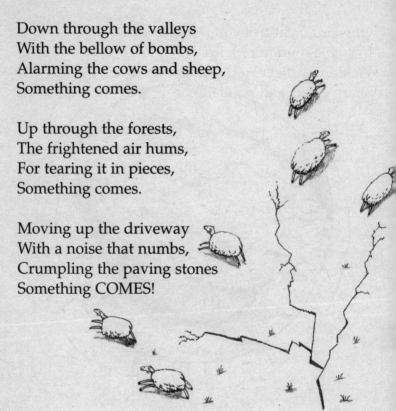

We Don't Believe

We don't believe in ghosts, Child,
We don't believe in ghosts,
We don't believe in goblins, ghouls,
Or any of the hosts

Of weird creatures you read about,
In comics and fairy tales,
We don't believe in things with fangs,
Sharp claws and pointed tails

Which are said to visit folk asleep,
And steal babies away,
We don't believe in changelings,
Or trolls that force you to obey

Their many evil wishes,
Who can bind you to their will,
We don't believe in leprechauns,
And we don't believe there's a hill

Where lords and ladies dance all night,
And disappear at dawn,
We don't believe in the naiad,
The dryad, or the faun

Who lurk in streams and forest trees,
Or fearsome creatures of the night,
We don't believe in vampires
Who creep inside and bite

You when you're sleeping,
And suck you dry of blood,
We don't believe in children
Living in a wood

Whose feet are turned behind them,
And whose piteous calls
Will slyly lure you to your death.
We don't believe in walls

Covered in moss and lichen,
Concealing magic doors,
We don't believe in fairy folk
Living beneath your floors

Who crawl through your rooms after dark,
Who turn the fresh milk sour,
And we certainly do not believe
In the supernatural power

Of werewolves, zombies, dragons,
Or in houses that are cursed,
There's nothing in the cellar, Child,
So come on! . . . You go first.

Snake

Sneaky Mr.
Forked tongue Twr.
Caught my Sr.
When he Kr.
Gave her a Blr.

How to Ask for a Hamster
(for Tamara)

Mum, can I keep a snake in my room?
What did you say? Are you mad?
Well, Jamie keeps a snake in *his* room,
He got it from his dad.

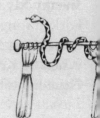

Will you buy me a mongoose, Mum?
I've played with one; it belongs to Maria,
It's really docile, can I please, Mum?
I don't think that's a good idea!

Can I have a pony then?
I could afford to pay for hay.
D 'you know how much a pony costs?
Japhet got one for *his* birthday.

How about a crocodile?
They sell them in Didcot.
I think that's where Chloe bought hers.
Can I have one? *Certainly NOT!*

I'll settle for a tarantula then,
It would be in a cage, of course.
Joshua has a tarantula.
Oh no! I can think of nothing worse!

What about a little monkey?
Tina has a chimpanzee.
Everyone in class has a pet,
Everybody except me.

You can have a cat, or a hamster,
You cannot have a snake or mouse.
No crocs, monkey or creepy-crawlies
I won't have a zoo in this house.

Okay, I'll settle for a hamster,
It's better than nothing I suppose.
Oh, there's the doorbell, must be Jamie,
We promised to go and play at Joe's.

Jamie, you were right, I tried it,
Just like you said, it worked a treat,
I'm getting the hamster, now tell me,
How do I ask for a parakeet?

The Plight of the Bumblebee

I can't make honey any more,
I've given up tasting nectar,
Yesterday I lost my job
As chief pollen collector.

I've done with flying from flower to flower,
Given up smelling the rose,
The perfume from the hyacinth
Now just gets up my nose.

I've just been expelled from the hive,
And I'm going now to pack,
The queen said that they don't need me,
There's something that I lack.

It's not my sting, my stripe, my wing,
Which makes me an underachiever,
The thing that's really hampering me,
Is that I've got hay fever.

Al Caprawn

He was the meanest marine creature
That ever was seaborne,
Sharp as razors were the claws
Of the fearsome Al Caprawn.

How the little fishes feared him,
How the shivers shook the frame
Of the shark, and how he whimpered
When he heard Al Caprawn's name.

Al Caprawn, Al Caprawn,
He's a gangster, he's a con,
You just know when he's around,
There's something fishy going on.

With pincers brightly flashing,
He paraded 'cross the sand,
Wreaking havoc with the smoking
Water pistol in his hand.

Once he grabbed the giant squid,
Squeezed it dry and stole its ink,
Then he marketed the liquid as
A brand new health food drink.

Al Caprawn, Al Caprawn,
He's a gangster, he's a con,
You just know when he's around,
There's something fishy going on.

With his henchmen Shrimp the Wimp,
Crab the Claw, and Lobster Reds,
He mugged the oysters, stole their pearls
Left them crying in their beds.

The news rocked the whole ocean,
As it went through the grapevine,
Only Al could do this wicked deed,
And on St. Valentine's.

Al Caprawn, Al Caprawn,
He's a gangster, he's a con,
You just know when he's around,
There's something fishy going on.

As a warning to the coral,
Al Caprawn once wrecked their reef,
Told them all, 'Pay me pwotection,
Or you're sure to come to gwief.'

'Hide your moustache,' sobbed the walrus,
'Watch your blubber,' moaned the whale,
'He's an evil little shellfish,
From his pincers to his tail.'

Al Caprawn, Al Caprawn,
He's a gangster, he's a con,
You just know when he's around,
There's something fishy going on.

Like Napoleon and Hitler,
Al got too big for his boots,
He spied a fishing trawler
And set off in hot pursuit.

Then he shouted to the trawler,
'You doity wat, give up that catch!
I will make you vewy sowy
That you twespassed on my patch.'

Al Caprawn, Al Caprawn,
He's a gangster, he's a con,
You just know when he's around,
There's something fishy going on.

'Those fish awe mine!' he bellowed.
'You'll be sowy you were bawn,
I'll teach you not to double-cwoss
The famous Al Capwawn.'

What a lesson to us all,
Not to act before we think,
Al in half an avocado
With a dressing that was PINK!

Al Caprawn, Al Caprawn,
He's a gangster, he's a con,
You just know when he's around,
There's something fishy going on.

Next Door's Cat – 3

Next door's cat ate my shark,
Though it took him quite a while,
So I've stocked the pond with something else,
A cunning crocodile.

The Tall Ships

I saw three ships, three tall ships,
Riding on the sea,
The waves quaked, and the fishes quaked,
And the wind sighed sorrowfully,
For on their decks, and in their holds,
Rode doom and misery.

I saw three ships, three tall ships
Anchored on the sea,
The wind refused to fill the sails,
The sky wept copiously,
For the berths were filled with pain and tears
And they hunted a new country.

I saw three ships, three tall ships
Speed shoreward from the sea,
And the trees moaned, and the birds fled,
And the land cried woefully,
For on their prows sat greed and shame,
And the death of history.

A Town Called Glory

Does the sun still shine on Glory,
Its warm rays still heat the soil,
Paint the rooftops with gold brushes
And make the tarmac boil?

Yes, the sun still shines on Glory,
And it still warms up the land,
And it makes the rooftops sparkle,
As it does the yellow sand.

And the stream that runs through Glory,
Does it sing as soft, as sweet?
And the fish and crabs that swim there,
Are they just as good to eat?

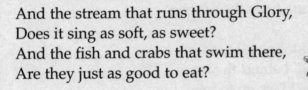

Oh the stream still flows through Glory,
But its song is slow and sad,
The fish and crabs still swim about,
But no one eats them, lad.

Do the fields ripen in Glory,
Do sweet corns and pumpkins grow?
Do the plums and cherries blossom
Side by side and row by row?

Yes, the crops are ripe in Glory,
Though they're not gathered now,
Fruits and vegetables flourish,
But I cannot tell you how.

Do the travellers stop by Glory,
Buy food in the marketplace?
And do strangers still leave Glory,
A broad smile upon each face?

Yes the travellers pass through Glory,
But they do not linger long,
And Glory's praises fall no more
Like manna from the tongue.

Does Old John still tend his cattle
On the hill behind the town?
And does Mary go to meet him
When the sun is going down?

There's a dark cloud on the hilltop
Where Old John once had his herd,
An old man roams the hill at night,
But he doesn't say a word.

A woman goes to meet him,
As the sun is going down,
Each day there's a new sorrow
In this poor, wretched town.

Cropover

There's a smell of burning in the air,
It's cropover, cropover,
It's August and this time of year
It's cropover, cropover,
The canefields have been reaped and there's
Just stubble in the places where
The cane leaves once waved in the air,
It's cropover.

There's a sound of music in the breeze,
It's cropover, cropover,
The drums shout BOOM! And the bamboos
    wheeze,
It's cropover, cropover,
The dancers leap, lunge, hug and squeeze,
Then pirouette with careless ease,
Cheers cascade from the tops of trees,
It's cropover.

Costumes sparkle in a halogen sun
It's cropover, cropover,
There's playing now the harvest's done,
It's cropover, cropover,
It's night, the feasting has begun,
Those pots of food must weigh a ton,
Now we will have some serious fun,
It's cropover.

Grandma, Bandana, an' Me

Mama tell me 'bout me Nana,
Granny Anna from Guyana.
'She's de sweetest, kindest Nana
That a person ever had,
But one thing about you Nana,
She just mad about bandana,
And the way she wear bandana
Is enough to drive you mad.

Bandana blouse, bandana skirt,
Bandana hat, bandana shoes,
Bandana bag, bandana socks,
A pure bandana Nana use.

Everybody know de custom,
An' is one dem hol' with pride,
White is the usual colour
That they use to dress de bride,
When you granny gettin' married,
People nearly dead with shock,
See her waltzing down de aisle,
In a long bandana frock.

41

Bandana veil, bandana train,
Bandana sandals, an' bouquet,
When him turn aroun' an see her,
Grandad nearly pass away.'

When ah go to Granny house,
As ah walk in though de door,
All me see was de bandana,
From de ceiling to de floor,
Bandana curtain pon de window,
De same cover pon de chair,
Bandana bedspread pon her bed,
She have bandana everywhere.

Bandana dishcloth in de kitchen,
An' de apron roun' her wais'
Bandana towel in de bathroom,
Granny's a bandana case.

She say to me, 'Ah have a present
Ah been savin' here fe yuh.'
She take out a bandana square an say,
'Now try this on Dudu.
You can tie it in a circle,'
(An she do it with a smile),
'You can leave a little hangin',
Now dat is the lates' style.'

Well ah look into de mirror,
An me heart just miss a beat,
De bandana pon me head look so
Beautiful an' neat,
Ah say, 'Granny ah look pretty!'
But she wasn' satisfy,
So the next time we go shopping,
Granny Anna meck me buy

Bandana skirt, bandana blouse,
Bandana hat, bandana boot,
Ah even buy meself a nice little
Bandana bathing suit.

She say, 'This is jus' the manner
That they dress in ole Guyana,
When my great gran was a girl,' an' ah
Believe her, I suppose,
So now when me go Guyana,
See me an me Granny Anna,
Lookin' like two walkin' banner,
In we bright bandana clothes.

Bandana blouse, bandana skirt,
Bandana hat, bandana shoes,
If you see we in the market,
Is bandana we a choose.

Baffled Turkey

Last night they brought a tree home,
They took it into the hall,
Now why would they do a thing like that?
I don't understand it at all.

Now they're hanging some tinsel upon it,
Some coloured streamers and balls,
And long loopy ribbons of twinkling lights,
I don't understand it at all.

There's a red and green circle on the front door,
And mistletoe on the wall,
And the farmer's inspecting a red and white suit,
I don't understand it at all.

Out on the porch they're erecting
What looks like a manger and stall,
With a stuffed donkey, a baby, and three kings,
I don't understand it at all.

Lately they've given me so much to eat,
I'm almost as round as a ball,
And now they are taking me up to the house,
I don't understand it, at all.

The Old Year's Lament

In January when I was young,
They made a fuss of me,
They welcomed me with singing,
Dancing and revelry.

On the first they celebrated
With a national holiday,
They yelled and cheered when I stepped in,
Shouted, 'Hip, hip, hooray!'

Everyone called me happy
As long as I was new,
And made long lists of all the things
That I would help them do.

And for the twelve months I was with them,
They let me hold their dreams,
I was the overseer,
Of countless plots and schemes.

It's true some lost their loved ones,
While I was in control,
But I tried to keep everyone happy,
And succeeded on the whole.

For those who loved excitement,
And violence, there was war,
Earthquakes, volcanoes, famine,
They couldn't ask for more.

And those who liked a quiet life,
Who preferred ennui,
I gave them those test matches,
And of course, daytime TV

I'm telling you, this human race
Is a very fickle lot,
They've heard the New Year's coming,
A fresh-faced, mewling brat.

They are planning the same celebrations,
We shared not long ago,
And not a single soul it seems
Is sad to see me go.

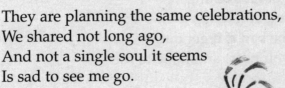

Secret

Can you keep a secret?
Keep it in your mind,
Don't laugh, don't talk,
Don't write it anywhere
In pen or chalk.

Ah tell me friend a secret,
Ah tell her not to tell,
Ah say is a special secret
So mek sure you keep it well.

Ah know dat it exciting,
But I asking you to try,
It would be bad if it get out,
So cross you heart and hope to die.

So ah tell me friend me secret,
From beginning to de end,
And that was de last o' dat secret,
She didn' even pretend

To keep it safe, she shout out,
In her loudes' voice,
'You mean you like that Malcolm?'
Now you tell me if dat nice?

She say she couldn' help it,
Say ah teck her by surprise,
Say ah really shoulda warn her.
Ah don't like to criticise

But when a person promise,
Take a oath right to your face,
She no ha' no right to broadcast
You business 'bout de place.

So ah ask me mum this morning,
Who can keep a secret most?
And she tell me, so me best friend
From now on is me bedpost.

Next Door's Cat – 4

Next door's cat finished my croc,
Yesterday at three,
I think that cat's a tiger,
And now it's after me.

Black Widow

I hear there's a spider wot eats 'er 'usband
I think that's well bad,
I'm glad I'm not a spider,
I wouldn't like mum to eat dad.

Sandwich

We goin' on a school trip today,
De whole class goin' to Whitney Bay,
Ah teckin' me ball an' bat with me
To play beach cricket, an' let me see,
Ah mustn't forget me new frisbee,
An teacher say to bring a sandwich.

She say to bring a waterproof mac,
An' a change o' clothes in a knapsack,
For it bound to rain, she guarantee,
An' half o' we gwine end up in the sea,
An' we mustn't forget, any o' we,
Teacher say, to bring a sandwich.

She say we can bring a can o' drink,
Ah will bring some fizzy orange, ah think,
Some gobstoppers ah can share with Lee,
(An' everybody else, probably)
An apple or orange, an, ah definitely
Won't forget to bring a sandwich.

Ah ask me mother for some bread,
Some butter, lettuce, an' some ched-
dar cheese, don't need nothing more,
An' ah just headin' for the door
When ah bump into me Granny Lenore,
An' she teck away me sandwich.

She say, don't know what you mother thinkin'
    'bout,
How she could let a growin' child go out
With one little sandwich alone to eat,
But don't you worry, chile, in this basket,
I have corn pone, chicken an' jerk meat,
You don't need to teck a sandwich.

Ah say to her, you don't understan',
Ah cannot teck all of dem things, Gran,
De whole o' de class will laugh at me,
She say, I do you favourite fricassee,
Ah tell her, Gran, teacher specifickly
Say dat we must bring a sandwich.

But she not listening to a thing
Me say. She waltz pass me an' den she bring
Out a bowl o' rice an' peas,
A whole hardo bread, if you please,
Ah was down on the floor, pon me hands an'
    knees
Beggin', give me back me sandwich.

Den Gran teck out a thermos flask,
Ah shut me yeye, ah fraid to ask,
But ah wonder what next she woulda produce,
She say, look, some nice soursop juice,
So gimme dat fizzy nonsense, dat's no use,
And she teck it, jus like me sandwich.

Gran, yuh have enough to feed de whole class
    dere,
She say, dat is right, yuh must learn to share,
Ah put something in for you teacher too,
And she pull out a bowl o' callaloo,
Ah ax meself, what ah going to do?
Ah only want to teck a sandwich.

No matter how me beg an' plead,
She was like a mad bull on stampede,
So wid chicken, rice an' hardo bread,
Me heart an' foot dem heavy like lead,
Ah wave goodbye to me street cred,
An lef' without me sandwich.

All day ah try to pretend
Ah didn' know dat basket, but in the end
Lunch time come an we all gather roun',
Spread some blanket on the groun'
An everybody settle down,
To open up dem sandwich.

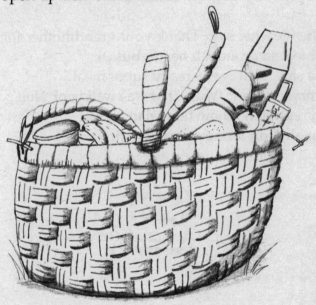

Teacher say, 'What have you got there?'
Ah pretend ah didn' hear,
But dat basket wouldn' go away,
So ah open it an' start to pray
Dat they wouldn' laugh too loud when ah display
What ah bring instead o' sandwich.

Well everybody yeye dem near pop out,
My friend Lee start to lick him mout',
So ah ask dem if dey all want some,
Dey look pon me like ah really dumb,
In no time we finish every crumb,
An dem all feget dem sandwich.

When teacher say, 'Thank your grandmother for us',
Ah feel so proud, ah nearly bus',
She say, 'That was a really super meal,'
Everybody say, 'Yeah, that was well cool, Neil',
An' yuh don' know how glad ah feel
Dat ah didn' bring – a sandwich.

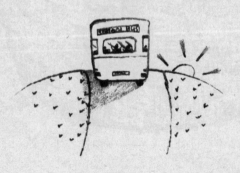

Eat Your Veg

Go on, try the artichoke,
Yes I agree they look
A bit unappetising,
But that TV cook

That you like, gave us the recipe,
And it doesn't taste too bad,
Well how about the peas then?
They're the best *I've* ever had.

What do you mean onions and peppers,
Are too crunchy when you chew?
That's the lamest excuse ever,
Just try a piece . . . won't you?

These tomatoes are full of vitamins,
Oh yes, you hate the seeds,
Will you taste the aubergine?
Then how about some swedes?

Daddy's done these parsnips specially,
Would you like a wedge?
Oh, come on, don't be difficult,
Mummy, eat your veg.

Just Wait

Ah goin' to live in a de forest,
Just meself an' me,
Ah goin' to run away when it get light,
Just you wait an' see.

Nobody goin' be there to tell me
Not to paint me toenail red,
Which dress, or blouse, or skirt to wear,
Or what time to go to bed.

Nobody goin' be there to criticise,
Ah goin' be on me own,
Nobody to frown an' make a fuss,
To groan an' gripe an' moan.

Me chair goin' to be a tree stump,
Me bed, banana trash,
Ah goin' eat me food out o' cocoa leaf,
Drink from a calabash.

Ah goin' brush me teeth with chew stick,
An' wash me face with dew,
Ah goin' use withes to make ribbon,
An' coconut husk make shoes.

Ah goin' swim like turtle in the river,
Swing from the highes' tree,
In fact, ah think ah goin' go right now.

But first, let me see what on TV.

Two Seasons

We don' have a Springtime like some folk
Who live in dem colder place,
but we have a time when de soft rain come,
an' tease open de seedcase
o' de poincianna and de trumpet tree,
An' whisper to de young cane to wake
when de guangu blossom is pink an' white
powder-puff, prettying up de earth face.
But not Spring like in dem colder place.

We no have no Summer when Springtime done,
no change o' season as such,
but we have a time when de asphalt bubble
in de hot sun, when yuh dare not touch
de tarmac wid yuh barefoot; when de heat is
a dancin' dervish who wi' grab yuh
an' spin yuh till de sweat is a river flowin' down,
an' yuh too tired fe do anything much.
But we don' have a summer as such.

We no have no Autumn like Europe,
we don' have de American Fall,
but dere is a time when de flame tree in the Forest
light de woodland like a fireball,
when de blue mahoe leaf dem turn bright bronze,
de almond look like it wearing henna,
when de nightfall flicker wid peeni-wallie,
an' grasshopper an' tree-frog call
to de moon. But we don' have Autumn nor Fall.

We don' have no winter wid snow an' sleet,
an ice like a carpet pon de grung,
but we have a time when de fee-fee twist
purple an' white up de road bank, an' young
tangerine an' ugli fruit swell an' yellow in
de gentle sun; when de cool breeze finger
draw de sweater round de shoulder,
an de sorrel tas'e tart pon de tongue.
But no ice like a carpet pon de grung.

We don't have de four season dem,
Summer, Winter, Autumn an' Spring,
but de dry season wid the noisy bees
an' de shrill call o' de cling-cling,
an' de sun turnin' de sea into a hot bath,
an' de grass bake so dat it crackle like parchment
under yuh foot; when de beach dem crowded
wid folk cooling off; de season when mango is
    king.
But not Summer, Winter, Autumn an' Spring.

No, we don't have four different season,
just two, de wet an' de dry,
an' in de rainy season de storm cloud dem
cover over de face o' de sky,
de road an' de river dem lose dem bank,
an' de hurricane dem sometimes come callin'
fe borrow de roof an' fe tear up de tree dem
like paper. But de earth always revive by an' by,
in de two season, de wet an' de dry.

A Tree Felled

Yesterday he was majestic,
Challenging the sky,
A crown of leaves, emerald green,
Strong limbs to hold the canopy.
Now those leaves lie dry and brittle,
Withered in the sun,
The branches that were arms outstretched,
Lopped, bundled up and gone.
The mighty trunk, a century wide,
Is prone, powerless, compliant,
There is no sadder sight, I think,
Than a broken, fallen giant.

Time

Time's a bird, which leaves its footprints
At the corners of your eyes,
Time's a jockey, racing horses,
The sun and moon across the skies.
Time's a thief, stealing your beauty,
Leaving you with tears and sighs,
But you waste time trying to catch him,
Time's a bird and Time just flies.

Total Eclipse

An eerie light haloes the treetops,
The nightingale ceases to sing,
The owl's eyes open, dilated,
Starlings tuck their heads under their wings.

A cold wind awakes from the waters,
Walks mournfully over the sand,
And the darkness, swift as a flash flood,
Covers the face of the land.

The earth holds its breath in wonder,
The silence complete, unbroken,
And there's a tiny glimpse of the way it was
Before the world was spoken.

Whose Dem Boots

Whose dem boots ah hearin', chile,
Whose dem boots ah hear?
Whose dem boots ah hearin', chile,
Whose dem boots ah hear?
Dem boots trampin' down de road
Dat fill me heart wid fear?

Gotta fin' me a hid'n place,
Whai! Whai!
Gotta fin' me a hid'n place.

Whose dem boots ah hearin', chile,
Comin' thru me gate?
Whose dem boots ah hearin', chile,
Comin' thru me gate?
Trampin' straight up to me door?
Tell dem please to wait.

Gotta fin' me a hid'n place,
Whai! Whai!
Gotta fin' me a hid'n place.

Whose dem boots ah seein', chile,
Stand'n by me bed?
Whose dem boots ah seein', chile,
Stand'n by me bed?
Waitin' dere so patient, chile?
Tell dem go ahead.

Gotta fin' me a hid'n place,
Whai! Whai!
Gotta fin' me a hid'n . . . Huh!

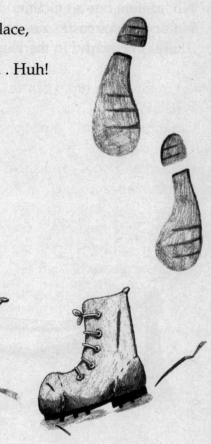

Silence

No grasses whisper, no birds sing,
No sound from any living thing,
No brooks babble, no branches creak,
No hunters cry, no victims shriek,
No dry leaves rustle, no creepies crawl,
There is no sound in the world at all.

Uncle Sam

Uncle Sam is six foot six,
Uncle Sam real brave,
When dem see him comin'
All de bad pickney dem behave.

Uncle Sam a expert
Pon ju-jitsu an' kung fu,
An' wrestlin' an' karate,
Nearly everyt'ing him can do.

Uncle Sam nuh fraid nobody,
Yuh cyaan scare him wid stick or gun,
But when him see a patoo,
Yuh fe see Uncle Sam run!

Mummy, are You Blind?

Mummy, please! For goodness sake,
You just stepped on my wedding cake!
No, that was not a pile of sand.
Oh! Now you've wrecked my new rock band.
They might have looked like three dead flies,
But that's 'cause you're looking with Mummy
    eyes.
Mum, don't sit there! Be careful, please,
You almost squashed the biscuits and cheese.
What do you mean it's an empty chair?
Anyone could see that's a table there.
Aren't you going to say hello to Sue?
She's standing right there beside you.
Here's your chocolate cake, hope you enjoy it.
Mum, it just *looks* like a dog biscuit.
Oh, Mummy, that's not Rover's bowl,
It's the golden platter that the prince stole
From the giant king. Oh, never mind,
You can go now. It was very kind
Of you to offer to play with me,
But I think I'll just have Sue for tea.
You'd better go and have your dip,
Don't step on my sailing! . . . ship.

Why are grown-ups all so dim?
You have to teach them everything.

I Think Shushila Likes Me

I think Shushila likes me,
My little dove! I'm almost sure.

What do you mean she likes you?
She just showed you to the door!
Yesterday at break time
She whacked you on the head,
You asked her for a kiss,
She gave you a thump instead.
And when you sat in English class
And wrote her that long note,
She laughed loud when she got it
Told the whole class what you wrote.
The names Shushila calls you,
Would make a grown man weep,
She thinks you are a 'reptile',
A 'wimp', a 'jerk', a 'creep'
You think Shushila likes you?
That she is your 'little Dove'?

You're right, she doesn't like me.
That is not like, that's love!

I Hope Tomorrow Never Comes

I don't want to leave today,
Don't want to go tomorrow,
Has anyone got some extra hours?
I want a few to borrow

To add on to the end of today,
For today has been so good,
I cannot bear to have it go,
I'd bottle it if I could.

Then I could keep for ever
My fabulous birthday cake,
The party, the walk this morning,
The hedgehog and grass snake

At the bottom of the garden,
The new baby fishes in the pond,
The game of chess with my dad,
(For the first time I didn't come second).

Today has been so special,
How can I keep it here?
Perhaps if I don't go to sleep
Today won't disappear.

Of all the days I can remember,
Today has been the best,
But all that's waiting in tomorrow
Is another history test.

Goodbye (Cinquain)

And so
as evening falls
I close the curtains on
the empty bed. And shadows creep
inside.

Last Lick

Sue and me walk home from school together every
    day,
We play 'teacher' and 'hide an' seek', and 'tag'
    along the way,
But the best game is the one we always leave until
    the end,
Till just before we reach her gate, right beside the
    double bend.
Sue always get me first, but she won't get me
    today.
So as she reaching out her hand, I jump out of the
    way,
Then before she know, I stretch out my hand and
    touch her quick,
And as I racing down the road, I holler out 'LAST
    LICK!'

Hot Like Fire

Kisko Pop

When de July sun hot like fire,
Den I have jus' one desire,
To run down to de shop an' buy a
Kisko pop.

When de August heatwave frizzle
Up de leaf dem, an' not a drizzle
In de sky, I just feel fe swizzle
A kisko pop.

For kisko pop
Cool dung de body,
I take a kisko fe de heat,
Kisko pop taste better dan nectar,
Icy cold an' sweet.

When de hot sun start to burn me,
An' me belly start fe churn, de
Only thing dat will concern me
Is kisko pop.

Pirates

The night was as dark as an inkwell,
For the moon had gone visiting elsewhere,
But by the scuffling sounds around me,
I knew there was someone there.
By the grunt and the groan and the muffled shout,
I knew there was someone else about.

I knew he had come here to rob me,
Take my silver, my jewels and gold,
In the dark I had the advantage,
It was as if he had a blindfold,
But I was fine, knew the lay of the land,
Each bit as familiar as the back of my hand.

He was caught in the second trap I'd set,
I heard him yelp with the pain,
But he was getting closer,
And I reached for my weapon again,
I was willing to die for what was mine,
Ready to strike if he crossed the line.

So I stood there over my treasure,
On the X which marked the spot,
Then suddenly he was behind me,
My stomach twisted into a knot.
Then Dad came in, turned on the light,
Said, 'Time to stop playing. Sleep well. Good night.'

In an Aeroplane

The ground recoils beneath us as we speed away
    from Earth,
There's a roar like a volcano or a hippo giving
    birth,
Our silver stallion leaps the clouds, thunders
    towards the blue,
And we gasp in wonder at the sight that opens to
    our view.

The golden ball is slowly sinking, but before it goes
It sheds its light on blue and white and fashions
    bright rainbows
From drops of moisture – tears of mist and sweat of
    hurrying cloud,
Wispy trees stand to attention, ethereal and proud.

The cotton-candy mountains rise like titans
    on the right,
Below, the azure rivers lap the beaches of the night,
Wide fields of fleecy crops stretch for miles like
    virgin snow,
And softly shifting fingers point the way
    that we should go.

The Sun Is a Jack-in-the-box

The sun is a jack-in-the-box,
Springing over the rim of the horizon,
To startle the cockerel on the farm.

The cockerel is a town crier,
Loudly announcing night's passing
To the world.

The world is a sleeping baby
Who gently snores,
As she's rocked in the arms of the dawn.

The dawn is a beautiful woman,
Smiling warmly as she turns
To the sun.

The sun is a jack-in-the-box,
Springing over the rim of the horizon,
To startle the cockerel on the farm.

I Asked the River

'Why do you run?' I asked the river,
'So fast I can't compete.'
'I run,' the river said, 'because
I have some streams to meet.'

'Where do you go?' I asked the river,
'And what do you do there?'
'I go to the valley,' the river said,
'Where I wash the rushes' hair.'

'Why do you sing?' I asked the river,
'Such a sweet and happy tune?'
'Because,' the river smiled,
'I'm having lunch with the sea at noon.'

'Why do you laugh?' I asked the river,
'You'll share the joke I suppose?'
'I woke the mountain,' the river grinned,
'By tickling his toes.'

Then the river shuddered, groaned and sighed,
The song of the streams and the laughter died,
And it whispered sadly, 'I can't, I can't,'
As it limped along like an ancient aunt.

'Now why do you wait?' I asked the river,
'And why is your current so slow?'
'Something holds me back,' it said.
Its voice was faint and low.

'And is that why you're getting small?
Is that why you sigh?'
'I sigh,' the river said, 'because
I know that soon I'll die.'

'Why don't you fight for life?' I asked,
'You only foam and seethe.'
'My lungs are clogged,' the river moaned,
'And I can hardly breathe.'

'Perhaps a rest,' I told the river,
'Would help to clear your head.'
'I cannot rest,' the river said,
'There's garbage in my bed.'

'What's this garbage,' I asked, disturbed,
'Which is clogging up your sand?'
'Poisonous waste and wrappers like this,
Which just fell from your hand.'

Trees on Parade

The trees are on fire! The trees are on fire!
Call for the fire brigade!
The branches are blazing, the canopies flaming
All along the colonnade.
The trees are on fire, the trees are on fire,
That's the end of the trees, I'm afraid.

Don't worry, they're not burning,
It's just the leaves turning,
In time for their autumn parade.

A Rabbit and Her Little Ones

A rabbit and her little ones, fat balls of fur,
Were playing in the bush behind the house,
So innocent.

So innocent, they were quite unaware
Of the cat that watched and waited,
By the wall.

By the wall, death in feline disguise
Poised ready to strike,
Until I called.

Until I called to Tom they had not known
The danger, then they turned,
And fled.

De Bread Van

In a likkle village whey de soft moss peep
from under mango root, whey de mawga dawg
  sleep
eena de midday sun, de cock dem cuss one
  another
ova de house top, an' nobody no bother
fe shut de door 'gainst pryin' yeye
but meck de nosy breeze come in fe spy
under de tablecloth an' frilly bedspread,
dere's a van dat come to deliver bread.

Every Saturday when de sun teck a break,
de van climb de hill wid a rattle an' shake,
a tired cough, splutter an' groan o' de horn,
hardly at lunchtime, neva in de mawn-
ing. But by five widout fail,
wid a dawdlin' twistin' snakin' trail
o' blue-grey smoke, thin like a t'read,
de bread van come fe deliver bread.

De bread dem light, still warm an' yeasty,
dem cos' fifty cents or so, at least de
mangoose bread dem, long an' thin
cos' that. De sweet bread got currants in.
De man have bulla cake too, five cents each,
sugar-brown an' sweet, an' him will reach
to de highest shelf behind him head,
an' sell yuh some when him deliver bread.

Spice bun like dose in de city shop,
sprinkle wid cinnamon an' cherry on top,
water biscuit, crisp an' light,
if yuh lucky den yuh jus' might
get patty, hot wid scotch bonnet pepper,
de flaky pastry wrap up in brown paper,
but perhaps yuh prefer some toto instead,
when de bread van come fe deliver bread.

Den open de drawer, teck out de clean linen
fe wrap de bread, bun an' bulla in,
a clean tablecloth or a piece o' cotton.
Likkle baby wid not a scrap on,
ride pon de shoulder or de back
o' brother an' sista, runnin' up de track
to de road, whey dem hear up ahead,
de engine o' de van whey deliver bread.

Whey de village gawn? Which part it go?
All de likkle square house dem eena row,
instead o' mango, sugar cane, callaloo.
And a supermarket dat give 'better value'
siddung whey deh use to be a likkle stream.
De speedin' traffic sey was jus' a dream
from somewhey yuh visit when yuh go to bed.
Whey de bread van dat use to deliver bread?

De Familiar Tings

We go ova to Spain last summer,
Mum sey she fancy Marbella,
Bwoy, de food did really nice,
Me an' Dad couldn' stop eat de paella.

Mum get hook pon a spicy dish
Mek outa fish that we buy a de seaside,
Me brother jus' order a Big Mac and chips,
Wid ketchup pon the side.

De year before las' we go a Cyprus,
Me an' Mum tuck eena moussaka,
Harry sey him no eat what him cyan spell,
So him only have chips and pizza.

We go to Paris one Christmas,
Mum put on ten pound pon her hips,
Even Harry haffe agree that him couldn' recall
When him eat a better haddock and chips.

Every year when we come back from abroad,
Mum sey, 'De sight-seein' was good.'
Me an' Dad always like de beach them best,
Guess what me brother like. De food!

Ten O'Clock Bell

Ten o'clock bell, ten o'clock bell,
Hurry up and bring break time because I can tell
Miss Wray's getting ready to call on me next,
I don't know the answers, I know she'll be vexed,
She'll slowly turn purple, and then start to yell,
So what are you waiting for, ten o'clock bell?

Is Chile nearer Australia or New Mexico?
When water turns to vapour where does it go?
Does acid turn litmus blue, pink or red?
Was it John or Elijah the ravens gave bread?
Whose book has a character called Little Nell?
Do you know the answers, ten o'clock bell?

She's turning to face us, eyes skimming my row,
She's staring at my face and finally I know,
What it feels like to be hypnotized by a snake,
Perhaps, ten o'clock bell, you'll toll at my wake.
Is that ringing I hear? Have you broken the spell?
Oh no, it's not you, is it, ten o'clock bell?

It's only the ice-cream van out by the gate,
Today is the one day you mustn't be late,
You know I am hopeless at general knowledge,
She's calling my name now, how will I manage?
I feel like a snail that has just lost its shell,
Oh, there you are, thank you,

'Miss, that was the bell.'

Maths Is a Great Problem to Me (Pantoum)

Maths is a great problem to me,
Regardless of how hard I try
My brain cannot access the key,
I can't add, subtract, multiply.

Regardless of how hard I try
My teacher will mark my sums wrong,
I can't add, subtract, multiply.
'Try harder, you're coming along.'

My teacher will mark my sums wrong,
There's not a lot else she can do,
'Try harder, you're coming along.'
In my heart I know it's not true.

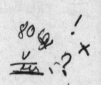

There's not a lot else she can do,
When I multiply eighty by four,
In my heart I know it's not true,
Sixty-two? Surely it should be more?

When I multiply eighty by four,
My brain cannot access the key.
Sixty-two? Surely it should be more?
Maths is a great problem to me.

94

Medusa's Problem

I have such problems with my hair,
You don't know the heartache it brings me,
I cannot wash or brush or comb,
For when I try, it stings me.

Heather

Heather wipes the young ones' faces,
Tucks them into bed,
Ignores the thoughts of better places
Sneaking through her head.

Whether it be rain in springtime
Or hot summer sun,
There's war to fight with dust and grime
And errands to be run.

Leather split in shoes and sandals
Must be patched. The door
Fresh graffitied by the vandals
Must be cleaned once more.

Heather gently bathes her mother,
Feeds her, combs her hair,
Thoughts of school she tries to smother,
Perhaps she'll go next year.

Benched

Hey, what is the keeper doing?
Why did he come out so far?
He was way off his line; it's lucky for us
They can't shoot and the ball hit the bar.

I'm the one to make sure we get a result,
I wouldn't make that kind of mistake,
Now why is he doubling over like that?
It looks like he's got stomach ache.

This could be my chance, his head's hanging down,
Oooh, he's just tying his lace,
Oh, nice feint, Arnie, now follow it through,
He's lost it! He just hasn't the pace.

I could have banged in that cross from Martin,
I could show them all how to play,
I'd have dribbled the ball straight through their
    defence,
Found the back of the net right away.

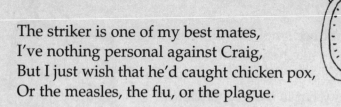

The striker is one of my best mates,
I've nothing personal against Craig,
But I just wish that he'd caught chicken pox,
Or the measles, the flu, or the plague.

I don't want to be mean or anything,
But one hour's already gone,
And if nothing happens to get someone off,
I'll never get a chance to go on.

What on earth is Simon Bell doing?
There was nobody there! What a prat!
I hope Sir noticed, now if that had been me,
I'd never have sliced it like that!

I don't really like being on the wing,
But I'd even go on for Fletcher,
Oh, look, Wayne is down, quick, somebody run
And call for the men with the stretcher.

Oh no, he's not hurt, he's up, worse luck,
Looks like he was only pretending,
I think I'll remind coach that I am still here,
I'll just try a little stretching and bending.

Wow, look at that Michael wallop the ball,
I could do that, honest, I swear
I kick further than Michael any day,
So why am I stuck sitting here?

Oh, great, coach is taking Emmanuel off,
I'm on, I'm over the moon!
Now I'll show them all how to play real football,
I'm on, not a minute too soon.

Don't talk to me, I'm as sick as a parrot,
I was doing good, I had such control,
I knew I had it in me to score,
But who would have thought – an own goal.

Troilet

The city is bustling,
But I love green fields.
I can't stand the hustling
The city is bustling
With thick, loud and jostling
Crowds. It wheels and it deals.
The city is bustling,
But I love green fields.

(for FS)

Associations

Moon, light, house, garden,
Rose, bed, home, warden,
Hostel, student, school, learn,
Exam, pass, work, earn,
Money, notes, book, police,
Court, judge, plea, release,
Breath, hold, ship, sea,
Shore, sand, castle, key,
Hole, mouse, trap, cheese,
Rind, orange, sun, bees,
Sting, nettle, forest, Arden,
Moon, light, house, garden.

Mary Had Ptomaine Poisoning

Mary had ptomaine poisoning,
The doctor felt her head,
Ptold her pto stick her ptongue out,
And sent her off pto bed.

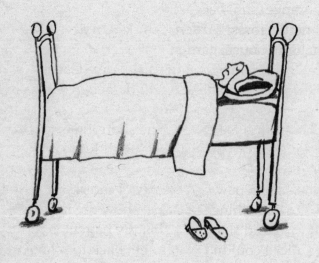

No Wonder

My homework – a story – is due, but not done,
We were told to bring three pens, I've only got one,
I've got a new teacher, the ogress Miss Blake,
It's no wonder a boy like me has stomach ache.

My rucksack's the one that my sister once used,
My haircut's the sort that keeps bullies amused,
My mum went and bought me a purple cagoule,
It's no wonder a boy like me dawdles to school.

My shoes were my brother's, they're noisy, they pinch,
During the summer I've grown over an inch,
But my trousers haven't, nor have my sleeves,
It's no wonder a boy like me underachieves.

The playground is heaving, the shouting is loud,
I've been asked to play football with Ron and his
    crowd,
And Joe's got a new bike he says I can ride,
Jake's got something special to show me inside,
Jean Brown said she thinks that my haircut is cool,
No wonder I couldn't wait to get back to school.

What's Wrong With Ephraim?

There's a new member in our family,
His name is Ephraim,
He didn't have a mum or dad
So we adopted him.

But he always looks so sad as if
There's someone he's longing to see,
And he walks round like there is a place
Where he'd much rather be.

I took him to the baths with me
Last week for a swim,
I thought a few lengths of the swimming pool
Would be quite good for him.

But he wasn't keen on the water,
I don't think he'd gone swimming before,
He made such a scene, the attendant was mad,
Told me not to bring him there any more.

Ephraim often snaps at me,
He's always in a bad mood,
Is it my company he dislikes?
Is it my home, or my food?

He doesn't seem to eat very much,
And he isn't growing strong,
Now I come to think of it,
Perhaps that's just what's wrong.

Let's see, this morning he had
Fresh cream with his shredded wheat,
A grilled kipper and a slice of toast,
And a piece of cake as a treat.

But he refused to touch it,
And the meat pie that my mum made
For lunch, he didn't like either,
'Cause he left it all, I'm afraid.

I'll have to talk to my mum about him,
For Ephraim is looking so weak,
I wish he could tell me what's wrong,
But of course, a rabbit can't speak.

Dreamless

The snake can't look forward to his dreams
   coming true,
Can't sing to his darling, 'Sweet dreams of you',
Can't dream of a Christmas, white or otherwise,
And when he is sleeping, cannot fantasize,
Can't travel in dreamland to faraway shores,
In his sleep cannot open imagination's closed
   doors,
No scenes beyond waking unfold in his mind,
And when he is sleeping, the snake you will find
Will not have a nightmare, won't wake with a
   scream,
For a snake is a reptile, and reptiles can't dream.

For Years I Asked Uncle Harry

For years I asked Uncle Harry
Why he wouldn't, but he'd just say
Maybe I will sometime soon,
I'm not in the mood today.

But I pestered my Uncle Harry
Till eventually he did,
And suddenly there was chaos,
The cat ran away and hid

Inside the rottweiler's kennel,
The fish all jumped out of the pond,
The parrot in its cage screamed, 'Let me out!'
And the blackbird in the garden went blond.

A wasp, just about to pierce Uncle,
Gasped, and then died in mid sting,
And the doctor's been treating me for shock
Since I heard my uncle sing.

The People Next Door

There are new people living next door,
They're as quiet as a comatose mouse,
We wouldn't have known there was anyone there,
But a blue light came on in the house.

And sometimes when they think no one's about,
A small head peeks out through the door,
But we never see an adult over there
They all seem not much older than four.

Our dog used to chase rabbits in the garden next
    door,
But he hasn't gone near since they came,
The ducks in the pond flew away it seems,
And that's a pity, they were getting so tame.

And the rabbits that were always hopping next door
In their dozens, have all disappeared,
In their garden, there isn't a bird or a bee,
Though we've got plenty, isn't that weird?

The vicar went over to welcome them in,
And now he is acting so odd!
If you ask him their names, or what they are
    like,
He'll just cross himself twice, smile and nod.

The postman who used to deliver their mail
Has gone away, no one knows where,
And that's such a shame because if anyone could
He would tell us what they're like over there.

The social worker went round to find out
Why the children weren't in school,
But we haven't seen her since, so I guess
She's probably visiting her mum in Blackpool.

Then we got a letter, pushed through the door.
Written on paper that just seems to glow,
Inviting us over for supper and games
Tonight at six. Do you think we should go?

INVITATION

One Thing

'You may have one thing,' they told him,
'One thing for company.'
He glanced around the small room,
It was bare, that he could see.

No table, chair, and though it was night,
No lamp, only the small window
Illumined the room, there was no bed,
He thought about it, then he said,

'I will have one thing here with me.'
'No furniture or weapons,' they warned,
'No tools or implements of any sort,
Ropes and ladders are banned.'

So he didn't ask for a knife or bed,
But something to eat or drink instead,
'And it's hot, something to keep me cool.'
'We said you could have one thing, you fool.'

He smiled and told them. Though surprised,
They got it from the store,
They gave it to him, shut him in,
Then locked and barred the door.

Next day they came to feed him,
But when they unlocked the door,
They found the cell was empty,
Save for some water on the floor.

They looked behind the door and then
They looked behind the door again,
They bit their lips and scratched their heads,
'He couldn't have escaped,' they said.

The door and lock were still intact,
No sign of forced entry,
So no one could have let him out
(They had the only key).

They're still baffled by the mystery,
They need your help now, so
Tell me what did he ask for,
And how did he leave? D'you know?

(Answer at the back of the book)

Shopping

One hour, that's all, ah tell me mother,
Ah can't stay out too late,
Ah jus' need to get a fountain pen,
An' a comic fe me mate,
Ah want to watch de match tonight,
So ah coming back by eight.
An' me mother say, 'Hol' on, ah coming.'

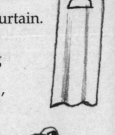

One hour, that's all, ah tell her,
We can't stay more than one hour,
We going get a pen, an' comic.
An' Mum sey, 'Ah want some flour.
An' while ah think I might jus' get
A new curtain fe de shower.'
An' me brother say, 'Hol' on, ah coming.'

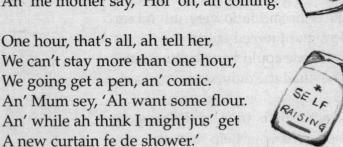

We only going out for one hour, ah say,
One hour before we come back,
We getting pen, comic, flour, shower curtain.
An' John sey, 'I need a rucksack.
But before ah go ah must set this thing
Fe video "Art Attack".'
An' me sister say, 'Hol' on, ah coming.'

One hour, ah shout to Rebecca,
Just one hour we gwine spen' in town,
We getting pen, comic, flour, shower curtain,
    rucksack.
An' Becky sey, 'Ah need a new dressing gown.
But ah don't think ah have enough money,
So, Dad, can yuh lend me ten poun'?'
And me father say, 'Hol' on, ah coming.'

Well, we go to de supermarket,
An' every aisle did have a food cart,
Dem was givin' out sample o' everyt'ing
From pineapple to artichoke heart,
Dad spen' half hour a-sample each sample.
Ah sey, Dad, de game soon start.
Him sey, 'Hol' on, ah coming.'

Next we go to get me brother rucksack,
An' him sey dat him need new shoes,
Well, John never learn how fe make up him min',
Him couldn't decide which fe choose,
Ah tell him, hurry up, John, before the match start,
We don' have no time fe lose.
Him sey, 'Hol' on, ah coming.'

Much later we go fe me sister dressing gown,
Dem was doin' a make-up demonstration,
An' when dem ask fe a volunteer
She jus' couldn't resist de temptation,
Ah sey, sis we don't have time fe dis,
By now me a-dead wid frustration.
She sey, 'Hol' on, ah coming.'

Mum see a nice shower curtain,
Exactly de one dat she need,
But she decide that she haffe find out
If it cheaper in Authur Reed,
Ah try fe tell her not to bother,
But she noh teck no heed,
She just sey, 'Hol' on, ah coming.'

Bwoy, we jus' headin' fe de car,
When, who yuh think we meet?
Me mother good, good friend Miss Jones,
That's when me admit defeat,
For me mother put down her shoppin' bag dem
Right dere in de middle o' de street,
An' sey, 'Hol' on, ah coming.'

We tell Mum we would wait in de car,
Ah feel me heart sink to de groun',
Ah know we wouldn't get back home now
'Til long after de match done,
An' ah sey next time a go shoppin'
Ah goin' on me own,
No matter who sey, 'Hol' on, ah coming.'

My Sister Thinks I'm Hopeless

My sister thinks I'm hopeless,
My sister thinks I'm dim,
My sister does not understand
Why I can't learn to swim.

I cannot do the backstroke,
I cannot do the crawl,
I cannot do the butterfly
Or the breaststroke, not at all.

My sister's losing patience,
She's shown me how to move,
To stretch my arms and kick my legs,
She says I must improve

Or she will wash her hands of me,
She says I'm a knucklehead.
But I think it's really very hard
To learn to swim in bed.

My Mate Fancies You

My mate fancies you like crazy,
My mate says you drive him mad,
My mate thinks you are the prettiest
Girl he's met, and I might add
That my mate's met quite a few girls,
He's a charmer, handsome too,
My mate's clever, and he's wealthy,
You're so lucky he likes you.

My mate wants to go out with you,
He wants to know if you are free
This weekend. There's quite a good film on
My mate says – at the Capri.
So will you be my mate's girlfriend?
Go out with him? You might? Yippee!
See you later. Oh, my mate's name?
Well . . . you see . . . actually . . . it's me.

Trick or Treat

Can you give us a sweet, Mistress?
Can you give us a sweet?
We've walked for miles in the freezing breeze,
And a hot toddy and some bread and cheese
Would stop the knocking in our knees,
For we're so cold, so cold.

Can we stop for a while, Mistress?
Can we stop for a while?
We've walked for miles with some aged crones,
And a spicy drink and some buttered scones
Would ease the shaking in our bones,
For we're so cold, so cold.

Can we sit by your fire, Mistress?
Can we sit by your fire?
We've walked for miles with owls and mice,
And a hot drink and toast would suffice
To thaw the blood which has
   turned to ice,
For we're so cold, so cold.

Why do you start and stare, Mistress?
Why do you start and stare?
Are you amazed by our sightless eyes?
It's just a Halloween disguise,
But we must be off before sunrise,
For we're so cold, so cold.

Today Is So Exciting

Today is so exciting,
I can't contain myself,
The clock is measuring out the hours
On the kitchen shelf.

Mum's cooking mashed potatoes
And sausages for sure,
As she's done each Monday night
Since I was three or four.

My granddad's softly snoring
In front of the TV,
A car just went by on the road,
The excitement's killing me.

A programme about train-spotting
Is showing on the box,
On the radio they're discussing
The price of shares and stocks.

Uncle Albert's telling me
For the sixty-seventh time,
How he collected postage stamps
When he was in his prime.

Outside and just across the road
There's a children's playground
Where an empty swing is swaying,
It's got me quite spellbound.

There's grass growing on our lawn
Which will not be ignored,
A fly's sitting on the table.
What makes you think I'm bored?

Late Again

Why nobody no wake me?
Whey everybody gawn?
Yuh mean to tell me I feget
Fe put the alarm awn?

Now is nine o'clock a'ready
An me gwine haffe run,
Me cyan find me school jumper,
Ah jus' gwine borrow me brother own.

Don' have no time fe breakfas',
Haffe jus' brush me teeth an' scoot,
No time fe pack me lunch box
Ah jus' gwine haffe grab some fruit.

An' hope ah can beg a sandwich
Or a biscuit off me mate,
Me outa here. Oh brilliant!
Ah hope me mum not workin' late

'Cause me lef' de key pon de table!
An' me feget fe comb me hair,
It mus' look like a bird nest,
But me no really care,

As long as me no late again,
For Mrs Morton sey,
She gwine give me a detention
If me late another day.

No sign o' de school bus dem
Outside o' de school gate,
Look like de lollipop lady
    gawn home,
Bwoy, me mus' be really late.

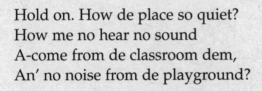

Hold on. How de place so quiet?
How me no hear no sound
A-come from de classroom dem,
An' no noise from de playground?

Whey de pickney an' de teacher dem?
Whey de dinner lady dey?
Oh no! Why nobody no remind me
Dat is de start o' de holiday?

Cookoorickoo
(Nursery Rhyme)

'Cookoorickoo,' de rooster a-shout,
'Cookoorickoo, blow de night light out,
For mawnin' a-come.
An' de moon gawn home,
Coo-koo-rick-coo-koo-rick-oo.'

Let's Go Play Football

Let's go play football, said Jez,
Let's go play football with Luke and Les,
We could see if Alan and Jason will come,
We won't ask Harry, 'cause I don't think his mum
Will let him come out, but Mike and Joe's might,
We could have a quick game while there's still
    enough light,
Let's go play football over the park,
Let's go play football before it gets dark.
And I said yes.

So we ran over to Les and we got him and Luke,
We went to get Jason and his dog Marmaduke
Chased me up a pear tree (Jez jumped over the
    fence),
And I skinned my knee and Jez lost sixty pence,
And Luke said it didn't make no sense at all
To ask the boy with that dog to come play football.
And I said yes.

So we went over to Alan's, he came straight away,
But Joe had some homework, so he couldn't play,
Mike came out of his house as we got to his gate,
He was going to the shop, but like a real mate,
He said he'd come play football with us lot
    instead,
If we'd go with him after to buy his mum's bread.
And I said yes.

We'd just got to the park when we met Harry
    Arthur,
He said could he play, Jez said, 'Don't think
    you oughter.
Remember the fuss your mum made the other day,
When we asked her if you could come over and
    play?'
But Harry said it was 'cause she remembered that
    we
Got him soaked in the pond and then stuck in a
    tree,
And right now his mum was off seeing his aunt,
'So,' he said, 'can I play? Oh please don't say I
    can't.'
And I said yes.

We picked our teams then; there was Jez, Luke and
    me
On one side and then there was Les, Mike and Harry
Against us, and that left Alan in goal,
The posts were Luke's jumper and Harry's cagoule.
So then Jez said to me, 'Come on, give us the ball.'
And then, 'Don't tell me you left it at home in the
    hall?'
And I said yes.

'Well, you better go get it then,' that's what Jez
    said,
'Honestly! I don't know what you've got in that
    head!
Well, what are you waiting for? And don't you be
    long.'
Harry asked if I wanted him to come along,
And I thought I could use the company,
Especially if Marmaduke was still under that tree,
So I said yes.

Well, we passed Jason's House, no sign of that
    dog,
And we were nearly at my house when Harry
    saw the hedgehog,
Just sitting there sniffling, by the side of the road,
And Harry said 'cording to his dad, the
    countryside code
Said we shouldn't leave hedgehogs where they
    might get hurt,
He said he would carry it inside his shirt
To where it was safer. Then he started to whine,
He held out his thumb and said, 'Is that a spine?'
And I said yes.

'Oh, it hurts,' Harry whimpered. 'It hurts quite a
    bit,
Could we go over to your house let your
    mum look at it?'
We hurried home then and my mum was real
    good,
She fixed Harry's hand and then gave us some
    food,
It was chips and hamburgers and then
    gingerbread,
'This will make you feel better,' that's what Mum
    said.
And I said yes.

Afterwards Mum suggested as we'd finished our
    tea,
We could go into the living room and watch some
    TV,
She thought there was something on we would
    both like,
A man jumping parked cars on his motorbike,
We dashed from the table, you should have
    seen Harry's face,
He's crazy 'bout bikes, he crowed,
    'Hey, this is ace!'
And I said yes.

Much later when we were halfway through a film,
Mum said, 'Where's your brother? I haven't seen
   him
Since half past four and his tea's getting cold.'
I stared at Harry and he suddenly looked old,
He said, 'Thanks, Mrs Jones,' we jumped up
   and ran out,
It was getting dark already, there was no one
   about
'Cept five angry boys. We saw Alan first,
Harry said, 'Think they're mad, fact they look fit
   to burst.'
And I said yes.

'What time do you call this?' That's what Jez
   yelled,
And Harry, the idiot, felt himself compelled
To answer that he called it twenty to eight,
Mike shouted, 'You imbeciles, now it's too late.'
(We could tell by the way his eyes popped
   he was hopping!)
'Too late for a game, and too late for my
   shopping!'
And I said yes.

'Yes?' (This was Jez.) 'Is that all you can say?
Yes? When we've lost two whole hours of play?
When we've stood round like idiots waiting for
    you!'
'Have you any idea what my mum will do,
When I come home without bread?'
    (This was from Mike.)
'Have you any idea what my mum is like?'
And I said yes.

'Well, it's done now,' said Luke, 'might as well
    make the most
Of what little light we have left. I say that lamp
    post
Should be goal. Why don't we keep the same
    sides.'
Then he turned round and started to mark
    with long strides
The size of the pitch right there in the street.
I stared hard at Harry, then I stared at my feet.
I felt like bashing my head 'gainst a wall.
Jez turned to me and said, 'C'mon, give us the
    ball.'
And I said, crumbs!

Some Lines About the Auk

As many people know, the auk
Is pitifully shy,
He'll turn bright red and shake with fear
If you should catch his eye,
And that's why no one sees the auk,
He only comes out after dauk.

Chickens from Space

Chickens from space, chickens from space,
Farmer Brown has a coop full of chickens from
   space.

There's a chicken with feathers all over its toes,
There's one without beak, just a long pointy nose,
There's one which lays only square, purple eggs,
One without wings, and one without legs.

They're chickens from space, chickens from space,
Farmer Brown has a coop full of chickens from
   space.

First the cows started dancing, the pigs all fell
   down,
And no one it seems could assist Farmer Brown,
Nobody could prop up his wobbly sheep,
And now he has hens he does not want to keep.

They're chickens from space, chickens from space,
Farmer Brown has a coop full of chickens from
   space.

How did they get here, Farmer Brown wants to
    know,
These hens without legs and these cocks that can't
    crow?
No one wants pork from the pigs in his pens,
And no one wants drumsticks or eggs from these
    hens.

They're chickens from space, chickens from space,
Farmer Brown has a coop full of chickens from
    space.

Some men in gas masks came and built up huge
    pyres,
But when they had put out the smoke from the fires,
These alien chicks like the phoenix were hatched,
Farmer Brown is now seeking a way to dispatch,

Them back into space, back into
    space,
Farmer Brown prefers chicks that
    are more commonplace.

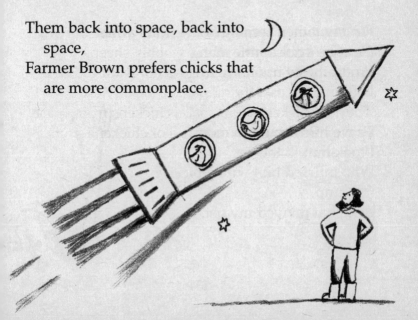

I Had a Pet Frog

Once I had a pet frog,
A pet frog green and warty,
He was the talk of the whole town,
The life of every party.

Whenever I took him for a walk,
The girls from near and far
All rushed out to kiss him,
My pet frog was a star.

I put him on my dad's chair,
So he could have a snooze,
And I nearly landed up in court
On a charge of frog abuse.

For my father, coming home from work
(And he's not a little man),
Promptly sat upon my frog,
Left him flat as a frying pan.

I gave him mouth to mouth,
I took him to the vet
Who inflated him with a bicycle
    pump,
And that revived my pet.

I put him on the radiator
As it was ten below,
But his skin went dry as the harmattan,
And his blood refused to flow.

I took him to the vet,
He soaked my frog in brine,
And after two weeks and three days,
My frog was doing fine.

Alas, my frog grew lonely,
Despite our special bond,
I introduced him to a lady frog,
Who lived in the village pond.

He visited her one Sunday,
A bouquet in his mouth,
But very soon he lost his way,
Turned north instead of south.

South led to the village pond,
North, to a busy road,
My frog was not familiar
With the Highway Code.

He did not look to left or right,
He did not wait to cross,
A milk float that was trundling by
Squashed froggy as it passed.

I took him to the vet,
Who prodded, pressed and poked,
Then shook his head and sadly said,
I'm afraid your frog just croaked.

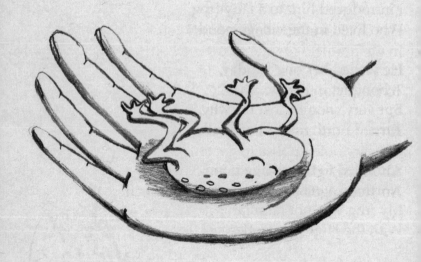

Nought Cuisine

When ah spend de holidays wid me sista,
Ah come back as thin as a rake,
De army could meck ammunition
Wid de things that she fry, boil an' bake.

Mash potato like reinforce plastic,
Her dumplin' is like a golf ball,
Ah try to taste de beef gravy,
But de knife couldn' cut it at all.

Her chicken soup stand to attention
In de middle o' de soup bowl,
It tas'e like she use a real toad
To make her toad-in-de-hole.

Ah not tryin' to say she cyan cook,
But jelly not suppose to go 'crunch'!
Ah always glad when de holiday over,
An ah can go back to eatin' school lunch.

On a Camel to the Moon
(Or Anything You Want, Son)

Some people like to fly high
In a small hot air balloon,
And some will get a thrill
From a train ride to Rangoon,
It's fun, I hear, to scuba-dive
Out in the Blue Lagoon,
But I'd like to ride a camel
All the way up to the moon.

I won't need the rocket fuel
So I'll save on the expense,
Inside a spaceship I have heard
The heat can be intense.
I get bad travel sickness
In a bus, a tram or train,
But if I could ride a camel
You would not hear me complain.

Oh I'd get the greatest pleasure
Snuggled in the camel's humps,
And he doesn't ask for too much,
Just some grain and sugar lumps.
He will skim through rocky craters,
Sail through desert and sand dune,
And is just the friend you want
On a long trip to the moon.

No, Dad, please not a new pet,
No chimp or young baboon,
I don't want to visit Egypt
Where you spent your honeymoon,
I want a birthday present
I will not forget too soon,
So can I have a day-trip
On a camel to the moon.

What Are We?

We're homes for ants and ladybirds,
We're hazel's ponytails,
Sometimes we're smooth, sometimes we're furred,
We're snakes with light green scales.
You'll find us very similar
To a sausage in our form,
Although our name suggests soft fur
We will not keep you warm.
We're avocado caterpillars,
And when we die you'll see
A tasty snack we've left for you,
So tell us, what are we?

(Answer at the back of the book)

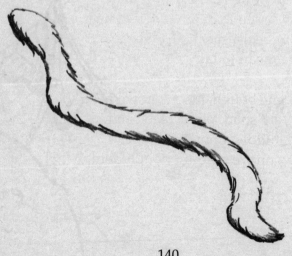

Don' Ride No Coconut Bough Down Dere

Papa face serious, him say, 'Dere's no way,
Ah want any o' yuh to go out an' play
An' mash up me yam hill dem down dey,
Specially wid unoo coconut bough.'

De hill so steep an' long an' slippery,
We could hear dat hill a-call out to we,
We could hear it a-say, 'Come slide down me,
Yuh know yuh want to do it now.'

De yam vine dem twist roun' de hog plum tree,
Dem turn dem likkle face to we,
Dem say to Lainey, Bonnie an' to me,
'Memba whey yuh fada say.'

De coconut bough dem waitin' dere
Say, 'Don' lissen to dem vine, yuh hear,
Yuh puppa really mean nex' year,
Him neva mean today.'

We fin' some bough, jus' what we need,
Head big an' solid, perfec' fe speed,
Me in de middle, Bonnie in de lead,
We jump pon we coconut bough dem.

An' den we all begin fe race,
De breeze like razor pon we face,
We feget 'bout goin' slow in case,
We break off Papa yam stem.

De t'ree o' we an' de dog, Puppy,
Fly down de hill pass de pear tree,
Tear through de cocoa an' coffee,
We noh memba de yam no more.

Up de hill an' down agen,
Lean de bough into de ben',
We only see de yam vine dem when
We stop, 'bout half past four.

Dem lyin' lifeless pon de groun'
De hill dem flat, dem all mash down,
None o' we could meck a soun',
We didn' know wha' fe do.

De hill so steep an' long an' slippery,
We could hear dat hill a-call out to we,
We could hear it a-say, 'Come slide down me,'
An' we say, 'No, thank yuh!'

What Am I?

Although I'm golden as the sun,
No one has ever seen me,
I'm the one you call for when you need
Peace and privacy.

I'm sometimes asked for in a court,
I lurk around the grave,
But though I'm best of friends with death,
I am not very brave.

An earthquake or a thunderstorm,
Even a shout will shake me,
And please don't say my name out loud,
For if you do, you'll break me.

(Answer at the back of the book)

Neighbours

Let me introduce you
To the people on our street,
They're quite the nicest bunch of folks
You'll ever want to meet.

Dan Singh lives at number one,
He's a ballet teacher,
Next door is A. Manning,
The Pentecostal preacher.

That's Mitch Egan at number three,
He's from the USA,
Number four's the tailor and his wife,
Mr and Mrs Hemmingway.

The one outside of number five
Is chatty Miss D. Bate,
She's lived there twenty years now
With her shaky aunt Vie Brayte.

There's the local bobby, D. Fence,
Who married Miss Dee Skreete,
Homes and secrets are all safe,
With these two on our street.

We used to have another cop here,
One called D.C. Eve,
But he wasn't to be trusted,
So we said he had to leave.

That's shy little Miss D. Muir,
In front of number eight,
Next door is Mr B. Hind,
Bless him, he's always late.

Mr Isher at twelve is a cleaner,
And his first name is Paul.
Me? I live at number nine,
And I'm your friend, Noah Hall.

Today

Today I will eat my cabbage,
Today I will eat my sprouts,
Today I will swallow my cauliflower
And not spit a single bit out.

Today I will not hit my sister,
Today I will not call her names,
Like toad-face, spotty, walrus rump,
I'll let her join in my games.

Today I'll not argue with Mum,
When she tells me to tidy my room,
I'll not take my sword into her rose bed,
And chop off all the blooms.

Today, no matter how much I long
To sit on my brother, Percy,
And pummel him until he cries
(On his knees) to me for mercy.

However much I want this,
I will restrain myself,
Instead I'll listen to him read,
Help Dad put up a shelf.

I'll let Amy play with my gameboy,
I'll return her tape which I hid,
Today I'll try to put right
All of the wrongs I did.

I will not give cause for complaint,
I'll not act like a twit,
For tomorrow's my birthday. I just hope
The presents will be worth it.

When Teacher Says It's Time for Play

When teacher says it's time for play,
And you shuffle out to see the day
Glowering at you through snow-filled eyes,
When scowling clouds handcuff the skies,
And the bully, Wind, with fists of ice
Is waiting with Sleet, his accomplice,
To rob you of each painful breath
With a frosted punch, when even death
Would be preferable to the constant pain
Of frozen toes and ice-capped brain,
When all through break you dare not linger,
For fear of losing nose and finger,
To hungry winter's spiteful bite,
When you get caught in a snowball fight,
Which leaves you shivering, your teeth chattering,
And muffled laughter and crockery clattering,
Direct your eyes to the staffroom, where
Your teacher's sitting in an easy chair,
Lazily sipping piping tea.
(Life is hardly fair, you see.)

You bend down to lace up your shoe,
And your knees have turned a purpley blue,
If you wonder 'bout this violation,
Of your right to warmth, it's regulation,
Children, they say, must have fresh air.
There's not much you can do, I fear,
Except imagine you're in a sauna,
And pray that spring's around the corner.

I Am

Where sun dances with the shadows,
Shifting like a hologram,
Where the dark and light join forces,
That is where I am.

When the warm air suddenly shivers,
When you feel there's someone near,
When a soundless footfall echoes,
It's my footstep you can hear.

As a thought, winged like a swallow,
As a sigh that's soft with love,
Like a wish, a hope, a prayer,
That is how I move.

The old man hobbling by on crutches,
The newborn baby in the pram,
The parson, pauper, prince and pageboy,
All of these, I am.

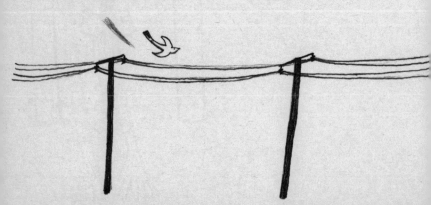

My Best Friend Is an Alien

My best friend is an alien,
Must have come down from the skies,
She tries to fit in, but I know
She's an alien in disguise.

My best friend is an alien,
I say it sorrowfully,
There are vital pieces missing
From her anatomy.

My best friend is an alien,
With tiny toes on her feet,
Her ears and nose are barely there,
My best friend's incomplete.

My best friend is an alien,
A changeling, swapped at birth,
She has two hands instead of three,
I think my best friend is from Earth.

A Skunk Stood on the Highway

A skunk stood on the highway,
Saw a monster tortoise with a shell
As big as a small mountain,
Heard its voice like a loud bombshell.

The skunk stood still on the highway,
Uncorked his odorous scent,
It was the only way, he knew,
To win an argument.

No creature could brave his odour,
Alas, poor skunk, farewell,
No one had thought to tell him,
That juggernauts can't smell.

Rover

Our pet Rover is fearless,
If it's necessary he'll bite,
So we know we are safe from burglars
When we go to bed at night.

Rover likes to chew a bone,
The butcher's his best mate,
He has a beautiful kennel
With his name on a brass plate.

He has dog biscuits with his meals,
As a kind of appetizer,
He thinks he's an Alsation,
And I don't make him any wiser.

For he's a first-rate guard dog,
His bark's such a moral booster,
I haven't the heart to tell him,
He's only a little rooster.

I'm Not a Kid
(Rap)

I'm not a kid, OK
I'm not a kid, I say
I'm not a kid.

Kids have horns,
Kids go ma-ay,
Kids live with goats,
And anyway

Kids don't wear trousers,
Don't wear shirts,
Kids don't eats lemon pies
For dessert.

So I'm not a kid, OK
I'm not a kid, I say
I'm not a kid.

Don't call me a kid
'Cause I don't like it,
Don't call me a kid, I'm a
Child, don't fight it.

Kids have hooves,
Kids chew the cud,
Kids nibble grass,
Kids eat rose buds.

So I'm not a kid, OK
I'm not a kid, I say
I'm not a kid.

Kids are animals
Like a gnu,
A cow, a giraffe,
Or a kangaroo.

I don't have four feet,
Not covered with hair,
Can you see a tail on me
Anywhere?

'Cause, I'm not a kid, OK
I'm not a kid, I say
I'm not a kid.

Oh, quick, Mum,
Look! See, over there,
'Flights to EuroDisney,
Extra low fare.'

Can we go, please, Mum?
No need to pay for me,
See, that sign there says,
'Kids Go Free!'

The Know-it-all

I think this child will sleep, she said,
And the little baby slept,
I bet that man will weep, she said,
And sure enough, he wept.
Just watch that woman sweep, she said,
And the woman promptly swept,
That horn is going to beep, she said,
And straight away it bept.

Pyramid

A
Stately
Chamber where
Vast treasures are hid,
Here ancient kings of Egypt
After they had died, were buried.
Grown used to pomp and circumstance in life,
Their every wish fulfilled by faithful servants (and by wife),
They left instructions that their goods and chattels travel with them.
Each jewelled headdress, golden sandal, every ring, each precious gem,
They hoped to use in the afterworld. The treasured goblet, plate and golden cup.
They never dreamt men with picks would one day find their graves and dig them up.

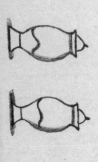

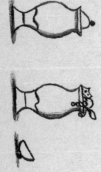

When Teacher Wasn't Looking

Sandy put paint in Chloe's hair,
Sandy daubed paint on Jemma's chair,
Sandy splashed paint everywhere,
When teacher wasn't looking.

Sandy whacked Joe, bruised his knee,
Sandy poured juice over Lee,
Sandy hit Rob, 'cause she could see
That teacher wasn't looking.

Sandy tied knots in Jan's shoelace,
Sandy just pulled a horrid face
At the teacher, Miss Lovelace,
'Cause teacher wasn't looking.

Sandy's been visiting Mr Mort
And he has put her on report,
Sandy was quite wrong when she thought
That teacher wasn't looking.

Underneath the Dead Plum Tree

Underneath the dead plum tree
Where red mushrooms grow,
Over by the silent stream,
There's a secret place I know.

I go there when I'm lonely,
I go there when I'm sad,
I go there when I've had a
Furious row with Mum or Dad,

And when Joan and Amy say
They do not want to play,
When they're mean to me and tell me
That I should go away,

Then nothing makes things better,
No one can understand,
Like the people that I go to meet
There in that different land,

They don't get angry with me,
They never scream and shout
Like parents, and unlike some friends
They don't boss me about,

They said that I should come and live
With them and be their child,
And we'd play forever by the pool
Where the red mushrooms grow wild.

So I've taken my small Bible
Put my necklace on,
The one with the small cross on it,
But when I went, they'd gone.

Glossary

a	at; to
agen	again
ah	I
an'	and
ax	ask
banana trash	the dried bark and leaves of the banana tree
ben'	bend
bulla	small, flat, round spice cake
callaloo	a leafy vegetable used like spinach; a stew made of callaloo, meats and seasoning
chew-stick	a vine containing a natural cleaning agent, chewed and used by hikers, campers etc. as a toothpaste and toothbrush
cling-cling	small bird named after the sound of its call
cos'	cost(s)
cropover	the festival which is traditionally held to celebrate the end of the sugar cane harvest in Barbados
cuss	curse
cyaan/cyan	can't; cannot
dan	than
dat	that
dawg	dog

de	the
dem	they; them; used to denote the plural forms of words e.g. 'han' dem' (hands), 'foot dem' (feet)
den	then
dere	there
dey	they
dis	this
don'	don't
dose	those
dung	down
eena	in
fada	father
fe	for; to
fee-fee	a vine which flowers around Christmas time. The purple and white flowers are partially dismantled and sucked by children to produce a whistling sound
feget	forget; forgot
fin'	find
gawn	gone; has gone
grung	ground
guangu	a large tree with flowers resembling small pink and white pom-poms
gwine	going; going to
ha'	have

haffe	have to
house top	roof
jus'	just
kisko pop	frozen pop in a plastic pouch
last lick	a game played by children in the Caribbean. The aim is to give the last touch before you say goodbye for the day. A lick in Jamaica is a smack/hit or in this case a touch
lef'	leave; left
likkle	little
lissen	listen
mangoose bread	long, thin bread resembling a baguette
mash	break
mawga	skinny
mawnin'/ mawning	morning
meck/mek	make; let
memba	remember
mus'	must
neva	never; didn't
noh/nuh	no; not; don't
ova	over
patoo	owl. The owl is believed by some to be an evil omen, its hoot signifying death
peenie-wallie	fireflies
pickney	child; children

pon	on; upon
puppa	father
scotch bonnet pepper	very hot Jamaican pepper
sey	say(s); said
siddung	sit; sit down
sista	sister
tas'e	taste
teck/teckin'	take/taking
toto	a kind of coconut cake
t'read	thread
t'ree	three
trumpet tree	a large tree with seed pods up to sixty-one centimetres (twenty-four inches) long. These pods make a sound like a trumpet when blown
unoo	you; your (plural)
wha	what
whey	where
wi'	will
wid	with
widout	without
worl'	world
yeye	eye(s)
yuh	you; your; you're (singular)

Answers to Riddles

Page 110: One Thing – The man asked for a block of ice on which he stood to reach the window through which he escaped

Page 140: What Are We? – Catkins

Page 143: What Am I? – Silence

Valerie Bloom

Valerie Bloom was born and grew up in Clarendon, Jamaica. She was enchanted with literature from a very early age; her work first entered the public arena when she won a national competition, and as a result saw her poem 'Mek ah ketch har' form part of the national festival.

Valerie moved to England in 1979. Here she began writing and performing regularly. Valerie studied English with African and Caribbean Studies at the University of Kent at Canterbury. She writes poetry in English and Jamaican patois for all ages. She has published several poetry books and two novels for young people while her work has been published in over 300 anthologies, including GCSE and the Caribbean CXC syllabi. As well as running writing workshops and courses, Valerie performs across the country and internationally; she has appeared everywhere from local libraries to the Royal Albert Hall. She is also a familiar voice on television and radio.

Valerie was awarded an MBE for her services to poetry in 2008, and has been awarded an Honorary Masters Degree from the University of Kent. She lives with her family in Kent and is inspired by everything around her. Caribbean life and culture remain a strong influence on her work.

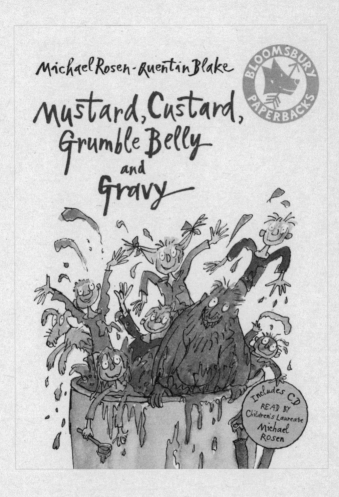

WICKED POEMS

'An outstanding collection of poems by poets
past and present.' FINANCIAL TIMES

Edited by
ROGER McGOUGH

Illustrated by
NEAL LAYTON